WONDERFULLY AND UNIQUELY MADE

Celebrating God's Design in Every Ability and Difference

Adrienne Isaacs

© 2025. Adrienne Isaacs.

All rights reserved. No part of this publication may be reproduced, distributed, or transmitted in any form or by any means, including photocopying, recording, or other electronic or mechanical methods, without the prior written permission of the publisher, except in the case of brief quotations embodied in critical reviews and certain other noncommercial uses permitted by copyright law. For permission requests, write to the publisher, addressed "Attention: Permissions Coordinator," at the email address below.

Cover and Interior Design by Adrienne Isaacs
All Scripture is quoted from The King James Version

Published by Adrienne isaacs
Printed in the United States of America

First printing, 2025.

ISBN: 979-8-9937784-1-9 (Hardcover)
       979-8-9937784-0-2 (Paperback)

Adrienne Isaacs
hello@adrienneisaacs.com

TO MY CHILDREN

GOD MADE THE STARS TO LIGHT THE SKY,
THE MOUNTAINS TALL AND GRAND.
HE MADE THE BIRDS THAT FILL THE AIR,
AND FORMED YOU BY HIS HAND!

YOU MAY FEEL DIFFERENT, SMALL, OR WEAK,
BUT CHILD, DON'T BE DISMAYED,
FOR GOD DELIGHTS TO SHOW HIS STRENGTH
THROUGH WHAT HIS HANDS HAVE MADE.

AND WHEN YOU SEE WHAT HE HAS DONE
HIS FAITHFULNESS DISPLAYED,
YOU TOO WILL LIFT YOUR VOICE AND SAY:

THERE ONCE WAS MOSES, MEEK AND SHY,
WHO STUTTERED WHEN HE SPOKE.
HE SAID "MY TONGUE IS SLOW, O LORD."
HIS COURAGE NEARLY BROKE.

BUT GOD SAID, "GO! I'LL GO WITH YOU.
YOUR WEAKNESS I WILL FILL."
THEN MOSES FOUND EVEN STUMBLING TONGUES
CAN DO GOD'S MIGHTY WILL.

HE LIFTED UP HIS STAFF IN FAITH
AND MIRACLES WERE PERFORMED.
FOR GOD WAS MOVING THROUGH HIS HUMBLED HANDS
AND WITH HIM THROUGH EVERY STORM.

SO JUST AS MOSES LEARNED WAY BACK THEN
WHEN FEAR, FOR FAITH, YOU TRADE
YOU TOO CAN LIFT YOUR VOICE AND SAY:

THERE WAS A GIRL NAMED LEAH ONCE.
HER EYES WERE DULL AND POOR.
HER YOUNGER SISTER SEEMED PERFECT, AND
BY EVERYONE SHE WAS ADORED.

BUT LEAH, SHE WAS CAST ASIDE,
UNFAIRLY OVERLOOKED.
OVERSHADOWED BY HER SISTER'S GLOW,
TO GOD HER PRAYERS SHE TOOK.

AND GOD SAW LEAH'S TENDER HEART.
HE HEARD HER QUIET CRY.
HE BLESSED HER OVER AND OVER AGAIN
WITH A LEGACY THAT WILL NEVER DIE.

WHEN OTHERS FAIL TO SEE YOUR WORTH
REMEMBER HOW LEAH PRAYED.
WITH GOD'S LOVE, YOU CAN FAITHFULLY SAY:

A LITTLE BOY ONCE TOOK A FALL.
THAT CAUSED HIS LEGS TO BREAK.
AN ACCIDENT THAT SHE DID NOT MEAN,
HIS NURSE'S SAD MISTAKE.

MEPHIBOSHETH WAS THIS LITTLE BOY
WHOSE LEGS NO LONGER RAN.
HE LIVED IN HIDING FAR AWAY,
FORGOTTEN BY MOST MEN.

BUT WHEN DAVID SAID, "COME DINE WITH ME AND SIT BESIDE MY THRONE,"
THE ONE WHO THOUGHT HE HAD BEEN CAST OFF WAS LOVED AND FULLY KNOWN.

SO, WHEN OTHERS RUN AND LEAVE YOU, STILL DON'T LET YOUR HEART BE SWAYED.
REMEMBER WHAT THIS BOY COULD SAY:

A MAN ONCE LONGED TO SEE THE LORD,
BUT THE CROWDS WERE FAR TOO TALL.
SO, INTO A TREE, UP, UP HE CLIMBED,
FOR HE WAS FAR TOO SMALL.

AND MAYBE SUCH A TINY SIZE
MIGHT FILL SOME OTHERS WITH SHAME.
BUT STRENGTH OR MIGHT, THEY MATTER NOT
WHEN GOD KNOWS YOU BY NAME.

YES, JESUS STOPPED AND CALLED "ZACCHEUS, COME DOWN. I CAME FOR YOU."
THE SMALLEST MAN AMONG THEM ALL FOUND LOVE SO DEEP AND TRUE.

WHEN YOU FEEL SMALL OR HARD TO SEE,
REMEMBER WHERE JESUS STAYED --
AT ZACCHEUS' HOUSE! -- SO, BOLDLY SAY:

PAUL PRAYED THREE TIMES FOR PAIN TO LEAVE, YET STILL IT LINGERED ON.
GOD SAID, "MY GRACE IS ALL YOU NEED. THROUGH WEAKNESS, I AM STRONG."

HIS THORN REMAINED, BUT GLORY GREW,
FOR CHRIST WITHIN HIM STAYED.
GOD'S POWER SHONE THROUGH EVERY GROAN,
HIS PERFECTING GRACE DISPLAYED.

"I'LL GLORY EVEN MORE," SAID PAUL,
"THROUGH ALL MY IMPERFECTIONS.
SHOW CHRIST IN ALL MY WEAKEST POINTS.
HIS GRACE IS MY CONFESSION!"

WHEN LIFE FEELS HARD OR STRENGTH RUNS OUT,
REMEMBER WHAT PAUL PROCLAIMED,
AND WHISPER THROUGH THE WEARY TIMES:

SMALLNESS, WEAKNESS, DIFFERENCES, TOO,
EACH UNIQUE TO PLAY THEIR PART.
HIS STRENGTH TO MEET YOUR EVERY NEED,
HIS GRACE WITHIN YOUR HEART.

SO, WALK WITH COURAGE, DEAR CHILD OF GOD,
THROUGH SUNSHINE OR THROUGH SHADE.
AND NEVER DOUBT THE TRUTH YOU'VE LEARNED:

YOU'RE WONDERFULLY AND UNIQUELY MADE!

Scripture References and Notes

God Gives Us What We Lack: The story of **Moses** is found in Exocus 4. Particularly in verses 10 -17, Moses tells God he is "slow of speech", Again in Exodus 6:12, Moses doubts that Pharoah will listen to him since he has "uncircumsied lips", a phrase that means he had unskillful lips, or was a poor speaker, Yet, despite these doubts, God reassured Moses that He will give him everything that he needed for the task.

God Sees Us When Others Don't: The story of **Leah** is found in Gensis 29. In verse 17 Leah is contrasted with her sister Rachel. Her sister was "beautiful and well favoured", but she was "tender eyed" which some translations render as weak eyed. God blesses Leah with many children. As Leah names her son Reuben (29:32), we see Leah's testimony of God's faithfulness towards her.

God Remembers and Restores Us: The story of **Mephibosheth** is found in 2 Samuel 4 and 2 Samuel 9. His grandfather, Saul, and father, Jonathan, were killed in battle which cause Mephibosheth's nurse to run away with him as a small child. During this escape, he was injured and became "lame of his feet". He then lived in hiding. Yet, King David remembered Mephibosheth, restored him, and invited him to dine "continually at the king's table."

God Knows Us By Name: The story of **Zaccheus** is found in Luke 19:1-10. Zaccheus was not liked by his peers because he was a tax collector. The Bible also says that his was of "little of stature" so much so that he could not see above the crowd and needed to climb a tree. The Lord Himself, called Zaccheus by name and went to his home!

God Shows His Strength In Our Weakness: The story of **Paul** and his struggle with a "thorn"is found in 2 Corinthians 12. The exact nature of Paul's thorn in the flesh is widely debated and there are many interpretations. Whatever the difficulty was, it is clear from Paul's story that removing a challenge is not always part of God's plan. Paul prayed for God to remove his thorn, however instead the Lord provided grace to sustain him.

For further exploration of each characer and helpful principles that we can learn from each story, be sure to check out **Wonderfully and Uniquely Made: Bible Study and Devotional Workbook.**